What Living with the Coronavirus Means to Me

An interactive workbook to help children and young adults, affected by the Coronavirus (COVID-19).

Jean Maye

Copyright © 2021 Jean Maye
All rights reserved.

ISBN: 978-1-8382356-2-8

Published by Mouse Chased Cat Publications

www.jeanmayeauthor.com

All rights reserved. No portion of this book may be reproduced in any form without permission from the author, except as permitted by U.K. copyright law.

Cover illustration and original interior illustrations © 2021 Steve Ince

Editing and interior design by Steve Ince

DEDICATION

To all the health professionals across the globe who have helped and supported patients with covid and to the scientists who have worked tirelessly to come up with the vaccines.

Introduction

There is no doubt that the coronavirus (COVID-19) has had a radical impact on everyone.

There will be many similarities in our experiences, fears and anxieties. However, we all have our own personal thoughts and interpretations of how we feel and how it has affected our lives. These are all heavy burdens to carry and we are not alone in this.

Living with the Coronavirus and what this Means to Me is an interactive workbook designed to help children and young adults come to terms with their experiences of coping with the virus. It is a self-help book, but it also encourages talking to others about your feelings.

Not being medically trained, I have not included any text directly about the virus. I have also tried to keep this workbook as simple and as generic as possible, to try and reach various ages who may benefit from using it. For those requiring additional or acute help with coping and mental health issues, please contact your doctor and the mental health support services in your area. They are always willing to listen and to help, so never be embarrassed to ask for support. We all need help during our lives, so if at any time during this book you feel sad, talk to a trusted adult about it.

I hope this book will help you come to terms with some of the impact of the coronavirus and the worries you have. My aim is also to help the start of rebuilding and adapting your life whilst living with the virus, and to introduce new hopes and aspirations for your future, whatever that may be.

With all good wishes,

Jean Maye

www.jeanmayeauthor.com

Completing this book

What Living with the Coronavirus Means to Me is your book to complete. You should complete it in a way that makes you feel comfortable and good about yourself. If younger in years, then I recommend you ask a trusted adult to work through it with you. As a young adult or someone in their twenties, you might want to still share with a parent or even complete this and discuss with friends. You might complete some things which are important to you now and leave other sections until later.

The important thing about this book is it is about and for you to record your experiences and feelings about what the impact of Coronavirus has had on you and your life. If at any time doing this you feel sad or upset, then talk to a trusted adult who you know will be able to listen to you and support you.

About the Author

Jean Maye comes from a background social care working with children and families. A published and best-selling and international author in this field, her interactive workbooks for children and young people have been a great success in helping many to make sense of their lives. One of her publications, *My Life and Me,'* has been translated into Japanese and used as a training tool in a university there.

In 2012 Jean achieved a master's degree in creative writing at Kingston University where she qualified as a social worker years before.

Jean writes full time and is also multi-award-winning screenwriter and filmmaker. She is now writing fiction novels.

www.jeanmayeauthor.com

Mouse Chased Cat Publications and Jean Maye, the author of this book, have made every effort to ensure that the information in this book was correct at press time, and while this publication is designed to provide accurate information in regard to the subject matter covered, they assume no responsibility for errors, inaccuracies, omissions, or any other inconsistencies herein and hereby disclaim any liability to any party for any loss, damage, or disruption caused by the use of this book, whether such loss, damage, or disruption results from negligence, accident, or any other cause.

The recommendation is that this publication is completed by a child or young adult with the support or knowledge of a trusted adult. The content of this publication is for informational purposes only and is not intended to be a source of professional advice with respect to the material presented. If such level of assistance is required, the services of a competent professional should be sought.

The use of this book implies your acceptance of this disclaimer.

My named trusted adult is:

....

CONTENTS

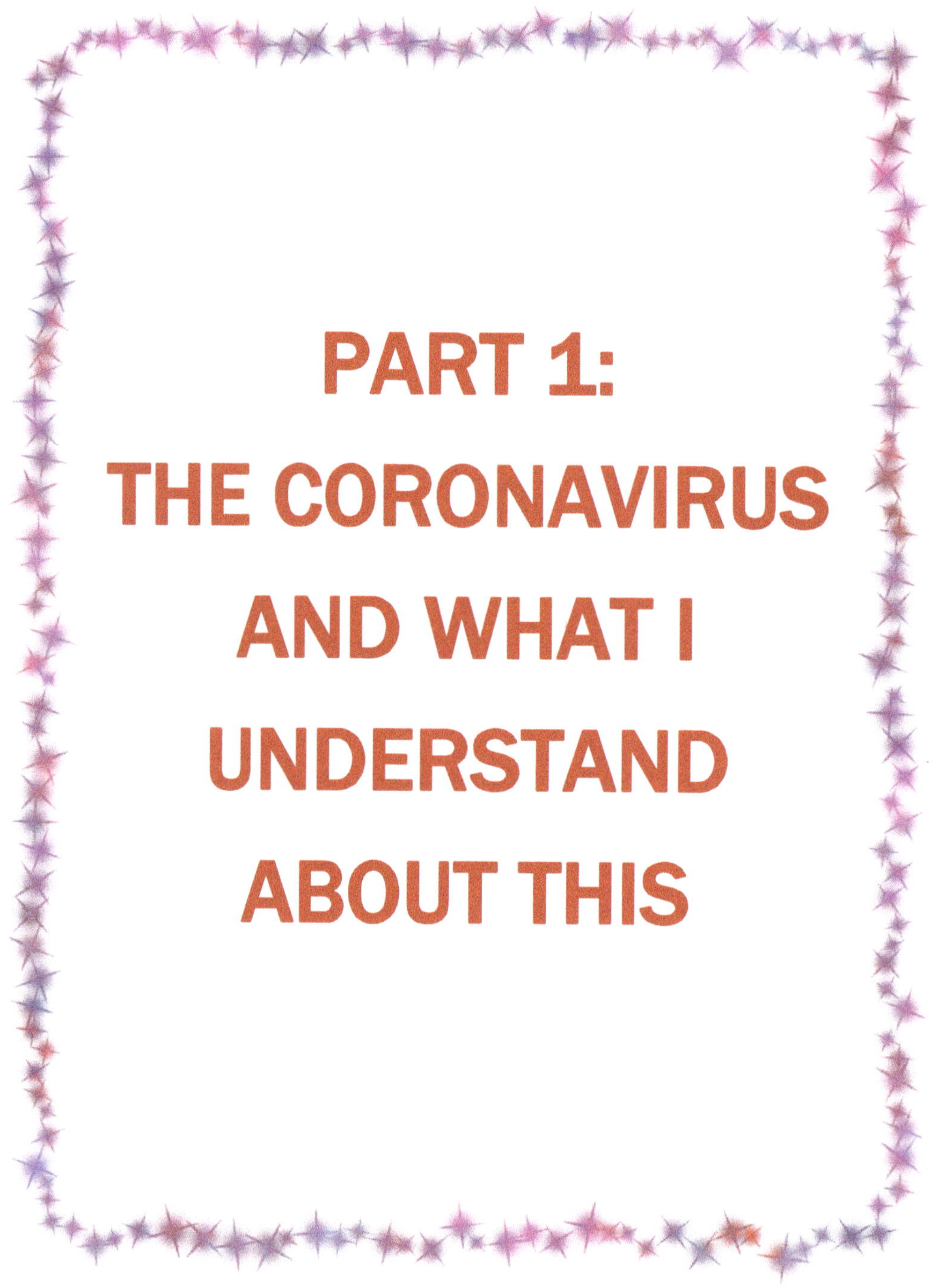

PART 1: THE CORONAVIRUS AND WHAT I UNDERSTAND ABOUT THIS

The coronavirus (Covid-19) is like having an uninvited guest who comes to stay for a long time. Although we want them to leave because they are interfering with the way we usually live our lives, we must learn to live with them until a time comes that they are prepared to leave. It is not easy adapting our lives, but we can try with the help and support of others.

Use the space below to write a few words about what you know and understand about the coronavirus.

Share this and discuss with someone you trust.

Remember, if at any time you decide to research information about COVID-19, there are a lot of sites with wrong and misleading information. In the UK, the ***NHS*** *site provides sound information, as does* ***The World Health Organization*** *which covers the rest of the world. Different countries will also have their Government websites for guidance.* ***Stay safe.***

People who have helped me to understand the coronavirus.

Date: ....

These are some of the things that they have said which has helped me.

Date: ....

Use this page to write or draw something about the first time you heard about the virus and how this made you feel.

Date: ....

Remember, if you feel sad, anxious, or alone, talk to a trusted adult or friend.

PART 2: ABOUT ME & MY FAMILY

Place a photo of yourself or you and your family in the frame below.

This photo was taken on .... by ....

Something I would like to say about this is ....

....

....

The people in my family.

Date: ....

Use the spaces below to say what you love about your family or the people you live with.

Date: ....

About Me

Use this page to say something about yourself.

Date: ....

Remember, if you feel sad, anxious, or alone, talk to a trusted adult or friend.

During the pandemic there have been restrictions in place and lockdowns to try and keep everyone safe and to stop the spread of the virus. The resulting situation has been extremely tough because you have not been able to see family members who do not live in the same household. Close friends can also feel like part of your family, so it has also been tough not being able to see them or socialize as you usually would.

Write about your experiences here and what this means to you.

Date: ....

Since the virus, we have all had to explore different forms of communication.

Even grandparents have been turning to Zoom and other ways of keeping in touch! In some ways this has proved a revelation!

Use the spaces below to record the different methods you use to communicate.

Date: ....

Use this page how you wish, to record some of the ways you chose to communicate with family and friends. Perhaps write about how this made you feel or about a funny experience.

One suggestion – not many people write letters any more but we all love to receive them, and especially grandparents. Why not set yourself a task to write a letter to a family member or friend this week and post it!

PART 3: CHANGES THE CORONAVIRUS HAS MADE TO MY LIFE

Throughout our lives we face many challenges that can change the way we feel or behave. Changes are sometimes what shape our lives. They can be physical and emotional changes like growing up. Perhaps from a happy event such as having a new addition to the family – a baby brother or sister.

Some situations arise that are difficult to cope with, especially the loss of a member of the family or a friend. Some changes are extremely difficult to understand, like the ones we have seen since the coronavirus struck.

The next few pages are here for you to write down some of the changes that you have had to make – or that have been made for you – during the pandemic. One obvious example is that adults and young people have had to wear masks to help prevent the spread of the virus and to protect others. Everyone has been affected by the physical impact of wearing them, and the emotional impact of seeing others wearing masks. I think we all agree, this is not a natural way of seeing our friends and family!

These are some of the changes the virus has made to my life.

In the first box below, write one of the changes in your life. For example, changes in your routine or lifestyle by not being able to see friends like you were used to. There are more boxes on the following pages. You do not have to fill these all in now. You can come back to them later.

What this has meant for me:

This has made me feel ....

....

Date: ....

In the box below, write one of the changes in your life.

What this has meant for me:

This has made me feel ....

....

Date: ....

In the box below, write one of the changes in your life.

What this has meant for me:

This has made me feel ....

....

Date: ....

In the box below, write one of the changes in your life.

What this has meant for me:

This has made me feel ....

....

Date: ....

In the box below, write one of the changes in your life.

What this has meant for me:

This has made me feel ....

....

Date: ....

Remember, if you feel sad, anxious, or alone, talk to a trusted adult or friend.

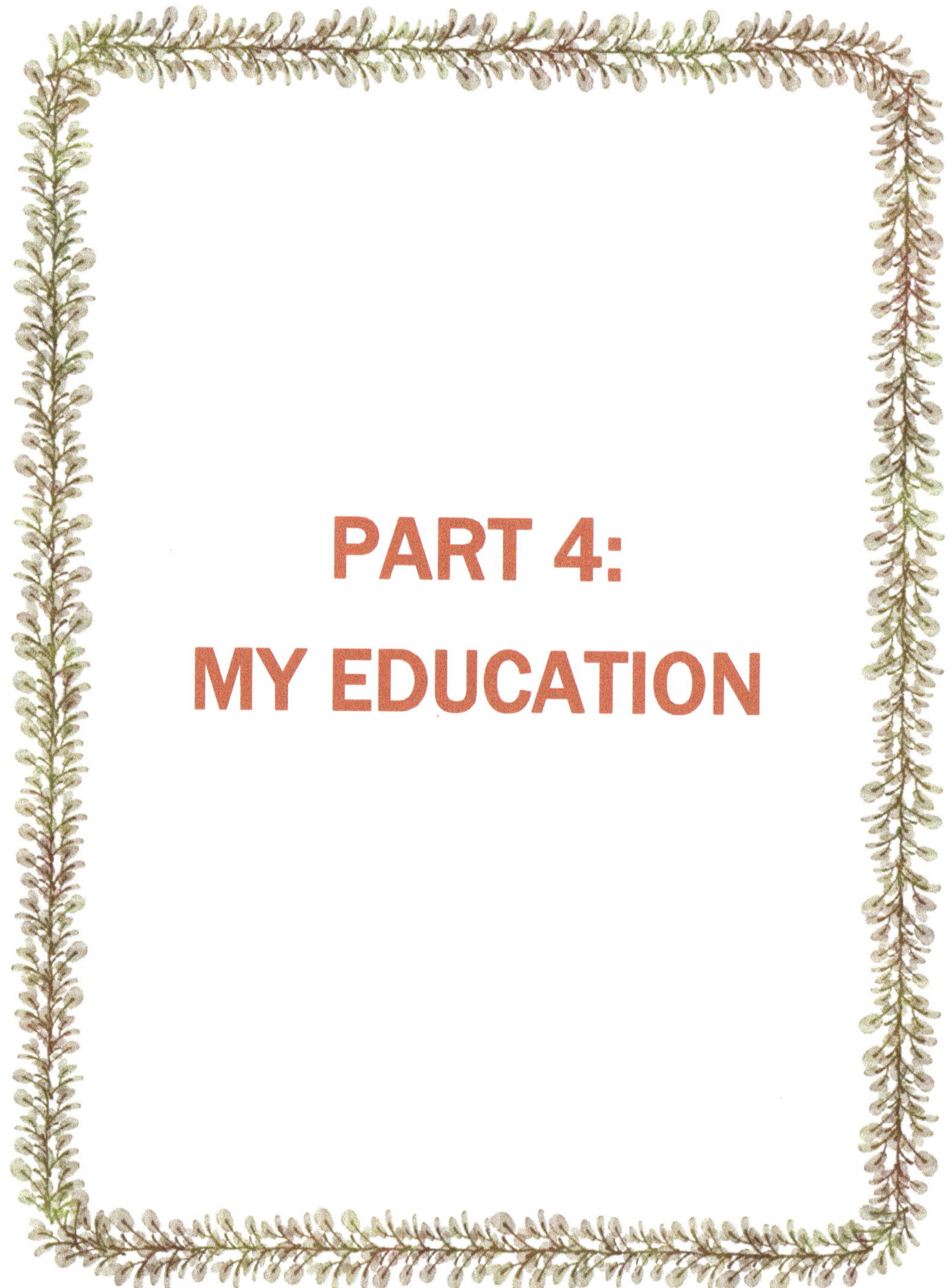

PART 4: MY EDUCATION

To help make the world a safer place and prevent the spread of the virus, you, other children, and young adults have helped tremendously by staying at home. Lockdown learning has been one of the biggest challenges for you. Even when the virus is contained and normal methods of studying resume, you may find it helpful to record your experiences and the effects of these changes on your learning.

Here are some of the things you might have experienced through lockdown and remote learning.

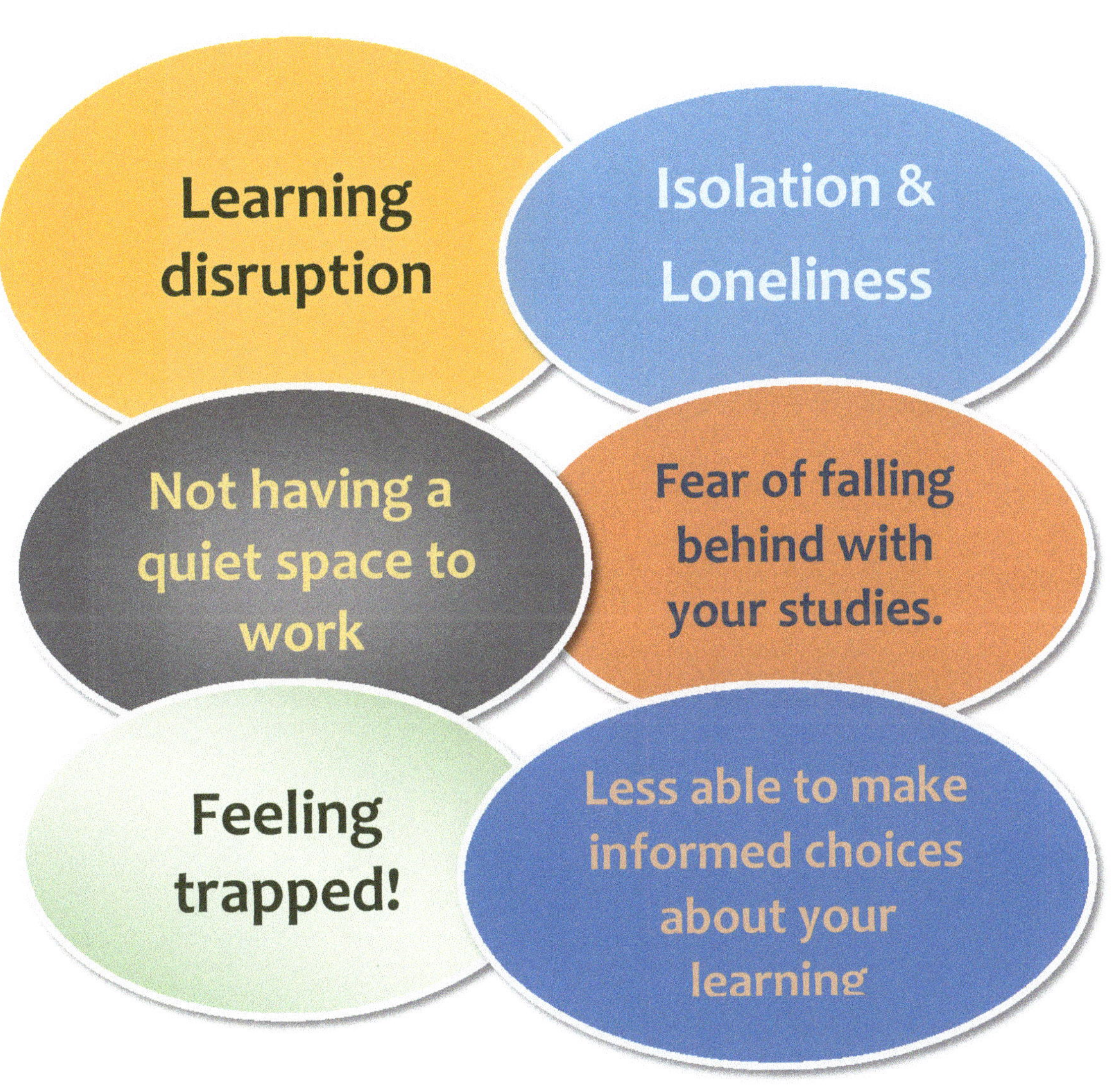

Use the spaces below to record key changes and challenges that you have faced.

Date: ....

Use this page write about the challenges you've faced with lockdown/remote learning.

Date: ....

With parents having to provide much of the home learning and support, use this page to say how remote learning changed things for you and your family.

Date: ....

Perhaps you might like to talk to them about this?

Remember, if you feel sad, anxious, or alone, talk to a trusted adult or friend.

Other things I would like to say about my education.

Date: ....

My transition between schools or university and what I would like to say about my experience of this .

Use this page to write, draw and to record other experiences about this.

Date: ....

What leaving school or university has meant for me.

Date: ....

Remember, if you feel sad, anxious, or alone, talk to a trusted adult or friend.

PART 5: CARRYING A HEAVY LOAD

My Worries & Anxieties

We all have worries and anxieties during our lives, no matter what age we are. Having worries can make a person feel very alone and isolated, even if they are surrounded by people who love them. One of the coronavirus' biggest impacts has been the way it stops us visiting our family and friends or socializing in the way we normally would. This has been a tremendous loss and had a huge effect on everyone's lives.

Sadly, we cannot control the world around us and right now we are even more aware of this – but we can change the way we are and how we live in the world.

This can be as simple as giving yourself a personal commitment to try and make yourself feel better and restore some happiness to your life by accepting the help of others. To achieve this, firstly you need to understand what is making you anxious or sad and acknowledge these things. That can be incredibly hard because we do not always understand why we feel anxious. So, it's very important to talk to an adult you trust and to try and write about these worries and anxieties.

Use the spaces below to write down some of your feelings, losses, and anxieties. If you don't want to do this alone, ask a parent or another adult you trust to sit with you whilst you do this. Perhaps you have a brother or sister who also has this book? If so, you could do this together.

My worries and the things that make me anxious.

Date: ....

Things that have made me sad during the coronavirus.

Date: ....

Remember, if you feel sad, anxious, or alone, talk to a trusted adult or friend.

My biggest anxiety is...

The person I am going to talk to about this is ....

because ....

....

After I talked to .... about my anxieties and the way I was feeling I felt ....

....

Use this page to write more about your worries and anxieties. If you don't feel like writing, perhaps you could draw a picture or write a poem to express how you feel?

Date: ....

Remember, if you feel sad, anxious, or alone, talk to a trusted adult or friend.

WORRY TIME

Talking about your worries and anxieties often solves the problem. But if they continue to weigh on your mind and prevent you from doing or enjoying other things, try setting aside some time during the day where you allow yourself to think about the things that are worrying you. Then as before, write them down in the spaces below:

Worry date & time: ....

My worries and what's making me anxious.

People I can share these worries with? ....

....

After I shared my worries with .... I felt ....

....

....

Because ....

....

....

....

Date: ....

Worry date & time: ....

My worries and what's making me anxious.

People I can share these worries with? ....

....

After I shared my worries with .... I felt ....

....

....

Because ....

....

....

....

Date: ....

Remember, if you feel sad, anxious, or alone, talk to a trusted adult or friend.

Worry date & time: ....

My worries and what's making me anxious.

People I can share these worries with? ....

....

After I shared my worries with .... I felt ....

....

....

Because ....

....

....

....

Date: ....

Remember, if you feel sad, anxious, or alone, talk to a trusted adult or friend.

Worry date & time: ....

My worries and what's making me anxious.

People I can share these worries with? ....

....

After I shared my worries with .... I felt ....

....

....

Because ....

....

....

....

Date: ....

Remember, if you feel sad, anxious, or alone, talk to a trusted adult or friend.

*If you need more space, you might want to use a diary and use this as a **worry diary** recording your worries and anxieties. Don't forget to record who helped you and what action you took.*

Staying safe is both physical and emotional!

PART 6: TAKING ACTION

The following pages look at what kinds of actions you might take to make yourself feel better. The first action, of course, is to talk about your worries and anxieties with an adult you trust. This isn't as easy as it sounds, so well done if you have been able to do this! It will make you feel a lot better.

During the book you have already recorded some of your feelings, emotions, and anxieties, and now you can use these pages to note some actions you can take to make yourself feel better.

Here are a few examples of actions that you might have come across whilst talking about your worries and anxieties.

SHARING MY WORRIES WITH MY FAMILY, DOCTOR OR OTHER TRUSTED ADULT.

REDUCING MY TIME WATCHING TV OR READING ABOUT THE VIRUS

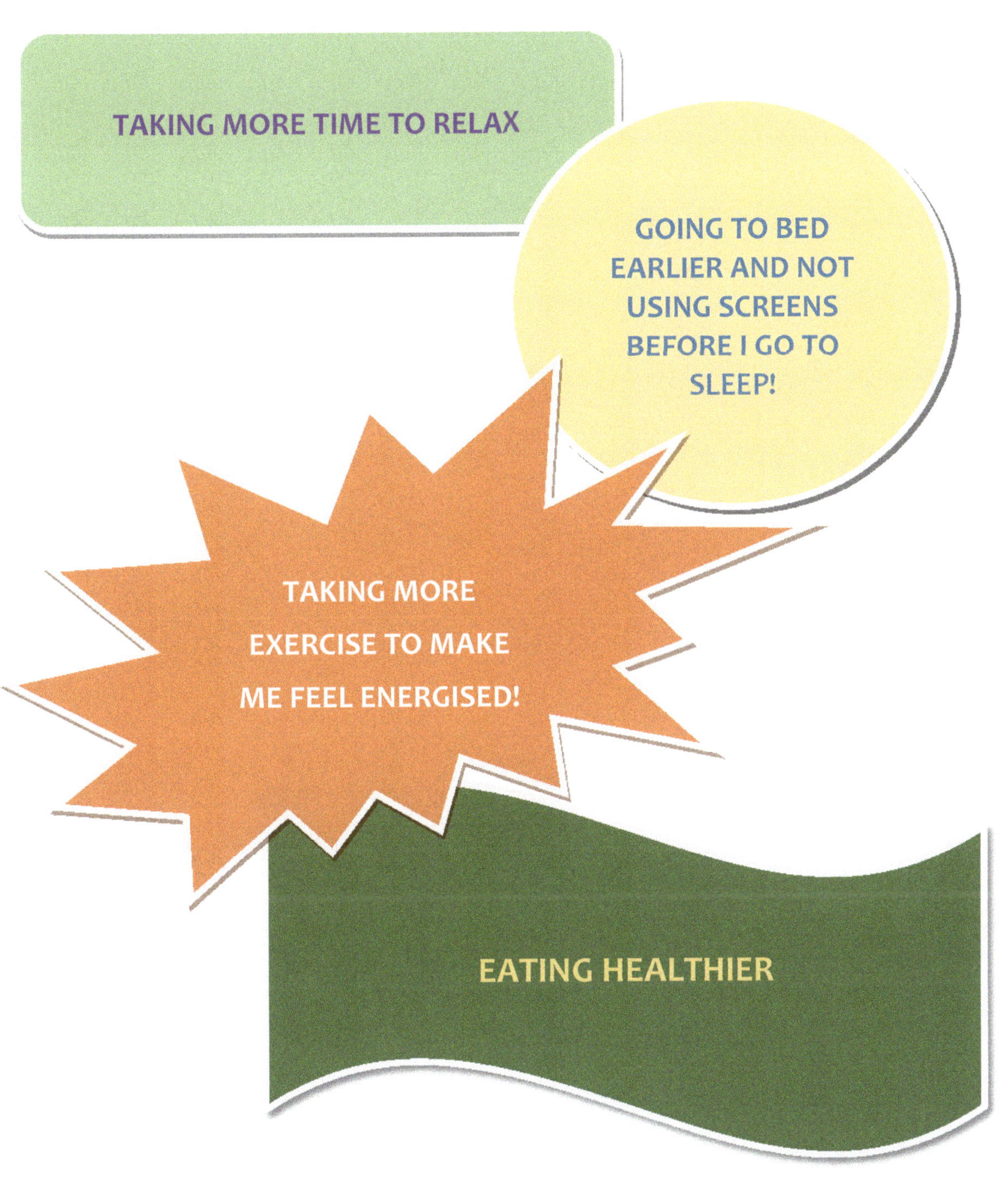

Remember, if you feel sad, anxious, or alone, talk to a trusted adult or friend.

Use the next two pages to record actions you have taken to make yourself fetter better. Be as creative as you like!

Maybe you even have an action plan?

Date: ....

Date: ....

PART 7: ALLEVIATING STRESS

Life is filled with stresses that can take away peace of mind, and these fit into the worries and anxieties that you have already been exploring. You may not be aware of this, but some of the actions you take to feel better will also help to reduce your stress levels. However, there are many other things that you can do to alleviate stress.

Following are a few suggestions for you to try.

Dancing is a cool way to reduce stress levels!

Explore nature, countryside, and parks in your area!

Sing!

Learn something new!

Perhaps chose a new recipe and cook a meal for your family?

Make yourself laugh – it works wonders! It can also make others you care about laugh too!

Remember, if you feel sad, anxious, or alone, talk to a trusted adult or friend. It's healthy to share thoughts, feelings and even the good things in life!

Use the spaces on the next page to record some of the things that help you to relax.

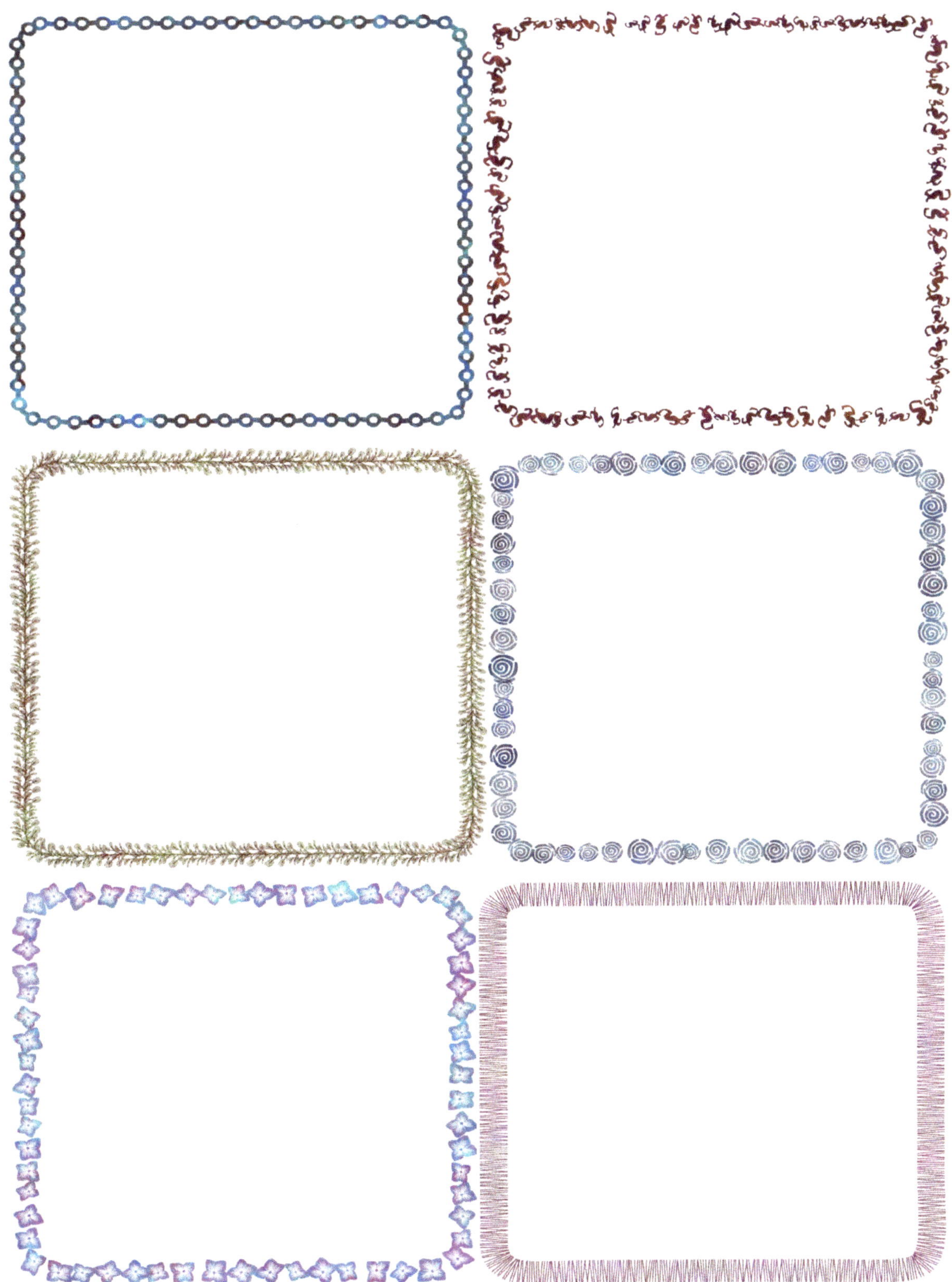

PART 8: THE GOOD THINGS

During the pandemic we have witnessed some extraordinary and inspiring events. Captain Sir Tom Moore is just one prime example of someone's courageousness. But good things don't have to be as big as this. They can be little things like clapping for the NHS/Health services in your country. This costs nothing other than a little bit of time and perhaps tingly hands depending on how hard or long you have clapped! These little actions have an enormous impact because recognition of help goes an awful long way.

Use the next three pages to record some of the positive actions and kindness you have seen, experienced or provided yourself during these challenging times. The last page has been left blank for you to use how you wish to record your good things.

You can be as creative as you like. For example, you might like to stick in a newspaper article, a letter or card, or simply write about your experiences.

My Good Things

Date: ....

My Good Things

Date: ....

My Good Things

Date: ....

People love to hear about good things so why not phone a friend or share these pages with a member of your family?

My Lockdown Memories

Date: ....

Other lockdown memories that I would like to record.

Date: ....

PART 9: GETTING CREATIVE

Use this chapter to be creative about your experiences during the coronavirus pandemic.

My Poem: ....

Date: ....

My rap/song about the coronavirus
(2 pages)

Date: ....

My Happy Story

Date: ....

Ignite your creative spark!

Make something new! Perhaps try a new recipe for a cake or a meal? Try a bit of woodwork, a new form of art, or even collect leaves and other snippets of nature and create a collage. Use the space below to record what you made, how and who with if anyone else helped.

Other Things I've Created

Date: ....

Sharing the love

Date: ....

PART 10: LIVING WITH THE CORONAVIRUS

These next few pages have been left blank for you to complete how you wish about living with the Coronavirus. You may want to write or illustrate how you found coming out of lockdown and how you felt when restrictions were lifted. Or about meeting up with family and friends again. The choice is yours.

Date: ....

Date: ....

Date: ....

Remember, if you feel sad, anxious, or alone, talk to a trusted adult or friend.

PART 11: LOOKING TO THE FUTURE

There is no doubt that your life will have changed because of your experiences with the pandemic. It is impossible to predict what may or may not happen in your future, but one thing you can be sure of is that **everyone has a future**!

Having aspirations and a list of things that you wish to do or achieve will give you something to aim for. It brings hope, motivation, and happiness back into our lives.

Things I'd like to do soon!

Date: ....

My wishes and aspirations for the future

My plans to help me achieve my wishes and aspirations.

Date: ....

My Joyful Rainbow of Hope

Date: ....

Whatever your future holds, I wish you and your family a happy and peaceful life full of positive adventures.

Jean Maye

You can find out more about Jean Maye by visiting her two websites:

www.jeanmayeauthor.com www.mousechasedcat.com

About the illustrator

Steve Ince is a freelance, award-nominated writer, artist and game designer. Among many other things, he wrote the book, *Writing for Video Games*, and the short film, *Payment*.

He has also written and illustrated a number of fiction books.

www.steve-ince.co.uk

www.ingramcontent.com/pod-product-compliance
Ingram Content Group UK Ltd.
Pitfield, Milton Keynes, MK11 3LW, UK
UKHW061955290726
14090UKWH00021B/1241